COURAGE AFTER CANCER

Rebuild your Physical, Mental and Financial Success

Megan Wolfenden

First Edition 2018

National Library of Australia Cataloguing-in-publication entry:

Wolfenden, Megan, author

Courage After Cancer: Rebuild your Physical, Mental and Financial Success

ISBN-13: 978-0-646-59830-7

Disclaimer

The people and events described and depicted in this book are for educational purposes only. While every attempt has been made to verify that the information provided in this book is correct and up to date, the author assumes no responsibility for any error, inaccuracy or omission.

If advice concerning legal or related matters is needed, the services of a qualified professional should be sought. This book is not intended for use as a source of legal or financial or personal advice. You are expected to be aware of any law that governs any financial and business transactions or other business practices in your State or Region.

The examples in this book are not intended to represent or guarantee that everyone or anyone will achieve their desired results. Every individual's success is determined by a number of varying factors which include his or her desire, dedication, effort and motivation. The tools, stories and information are provided as examples only; not as sources of legal, personal or financial advice.

Table of contents

Introduction

Cancer was the best, worst thing that ever happened to me. It might seem crazy to imagine a cancer survivor saying that, but it's true. And many other survivors feel the same way because their lives profoundly changed as a result of having cancer and they made those changes mean something important.

Survivors find a new purpose that drives them to create a life of meaning and contribution. You'll hear survivors talk about having a life plan for the next 5 years. They don't know what life will bring after that time, but they need goals and important things to work towards and look forward to. Compare this with people who have not had a tough diagnosis and you'll find less than 8% of those people set goals. Having looked death in the face means we are eager to live every day of our lives with meaning from now on.

This book is designed to show people who are newly diagnosed with cancer that life after treatment can, and should be, AMAZING.

Part one of this book is a brief description of what

happened to me when I was diagnosed with HER2 positive breast cancer and how I mentally processed and got through that time. My hope is that knowing someone is going through something similar to you will give you comfort, especially when I show you my strategies of how to cope physically, mentally and financially.

Everyone's story is unique and worth being told, but there are also similarities that will help you realise you are not alone. While the journey is difficult and takes time and patience, it's great to know that others have trodden the path before you and that amazing things are possible after recovery. I hope my story helps you see that you are right on track.

Part two is an extensive list of tools and techniques you can use to help you move forward in life and business to not only get back to the success you had before, but go beyond what you thought was possible, all while keeping your health great and your stress low.

In part three, you'll read about how people facing cancer went on to live with greater passion for the things that were most important in their lives. These stories are inspiring and will help you realise that incredible things are ahead of you once you get through this tough part of your journey.

An important lesson from survivors is that we know

with hindsight that our self-care was not enough of a priority before we got sick. After treatment, survivors talk about making self-care a priority every day and how self-care became vital for recovery and prevention. Most importantly, in this section you will read about incredible people who have found a way to make their illness a gift because of the new and wonderful way they look at life. Every day is special.

You'll love reading the interviews of the five wonderful people in part three. They are all at different stages of their journeys but all have their own unique positive spin on what has happened to them.

WHO IS THIS BOOK FOR?

I wrote this book as an inspirational guide for people who are going through or have been through cancer and are now ready to get back on their feet.

When I was ready to get back to work and start earning money again, I had lost my confidence and was worried about the difficult job of rebuilding my business. I wanted a new direction but I was scared. I was also desperate to start earning again after all the costs associated with having cancer, four operations, and 27 rounds of chemo.

My self-esteem had taken a hit and I was worried about

how I could live up to my original potential, especially because my energy was not back to where I needed it to be.

So many people are facing these same issues. I want to show you how your illness is only one part of your story and you can use your experiences to inspire others, motivate yourself and help your loved ones see that your illness can be the *best, worst thing that has ever happened to you.*

This book will show you the path to staying positive and rebuilding your life – physically, mentally and financially – while staying motivated to live your best life stress-free.

HOW TO USE THIS BOOK

Each of the three parts of this book can be read independently. If you want some quick inspiration to keep you moving forward and not dwelling on the present, go straight to part two and find a tool you can focus on to feel better and create your new future.

In that section, you'll get practical ideas for getting yourself back on track in all areas of your life. I walk you through step by step guides in areas that may be alluding you right now. The more you can look at what's holding you back and objectively adjust those areas, the quicker you will find recovery in all areas of your life.

Use these tools when you find you need a new skill. Try to add a new practise every week to help you build on your success and mindset.

My ultimate goal is to help you live a happier, more fulfilled life. As well as everything you'll learn in this book, I also develop individual life programs based on your personal goals and passion to help you reach success during this difficult time.

To book a free strategy session with me click here or click on the QR code below:

PART ONE

MY JOURNEY

THE DIAGNOSIS

My 81-year-old Mother-in-Law had quite a large lump in her breast. After telling us, she immediately went for all the tests. My husband took her to most of her appointments but I took her to the biopsy. The Doctor asked me to go into the room because he wanted to inform her it was cancer even before the biopsy results came back. We were both shocked and frightened. More specialist appointments followed and her operation was scheduled.

In the meantime, I booked myself in for a mammogram. When I was called back for further investigation, I was convinced it would be the usual "thick tissue" that was causing concern and everything would be fine. That's why I went to the appointment by myself. But as the technician was setting up for the ultrasound-guided biopsy, the doctor walked in and the technician said to the doctor, "It's not a cyst."

That's when I knew it was cancer.

My husband had both his mother and his wife diagnosed with breast cancer in the same month – November 2017.

Just to give you an understanding of what else was going on, my Dad was having radiation for a sarcoma on his arm but had to delay some of that for an urgent pacemaker to be put in. My Mother had also told me she thought a recurring cancer had started growing again. To say it was a stressful and surreal time is an understatement.

On Sunday 26th November 2017, I started an intensive 7-day coaching program to advance my business coaching skills and earn a certification. On the Monday night, one of my best mates, who is also my GP, was waiting outside my house knowing I was getting home late and the rest of the family were home. When I arrived home and saw him waiting my heart sank. No words were necessary. I walked in the door and saw my husband, Anthony, and then Dr Chris followed me in. Seeing us both, Anthony instantly knew my diagnosis too.

The three of us flopped on the floor, quite silent. Dr Chris put the report on the floor between us and we all made small talk for as long as we could. He had booked all my tests and scans and doctors' appointments for me before I even got home to the news. Everything was crammed into that week so we could find out everything we needed to know as soon as possible. We weren't ready to tell the kids or anyone else just then.

I didn't sleep well that night but I don't think I cried.

The next morning, I went back to my course and explained to the facilitator what had happened and he gave me the option to come and go as needed. Because my scans were all in the same area, I was able to leave the course for my appointments and I still got a lot of the course done. Because it was a coaching course that contained a lot of life coaching skills training, I was with an incredible group of people that week. I think this was a great way to keep my mind focused on other things while I was learning about my treatment and the exact type of cancer I had.

Interestingly, on the Wednesday we had a photo shoot on the beach to get our branding photos done as part of the course. It was the last lot of photos I had done before I lost my hair and they were great. It's so nice to have professional photos from that time. I can't really use them now as my long blond hair has gone away. This was cause for some stress and heartache later on.

We had booked a three-generation family cruise over Christmas. I didn't think this opportunity would present itself ever again and so I was determined to go ahead with the trip. The group consisted of my two teenage boys, my Mother, my Mother-in-law, my husband and me. Given the state of health of three of us at the time, I didn't want to pass up this opportunity. The trip was a cruise from Sydney, around New Zealand and back to Sydney over eight nights.

My Mother-in-Law had recovered enough from her mastectomy and my surgeon agreed to operate on me the day after we got back from the cruise (provided I didn't pick up any nasty cruise illnesses), so we made it work. Incidentally, my doctor agreed to operate on 30th December which was a Saturday, so I was very lucky it all came together. He was going away in January so we definitely needed to juggle everything if we were still going to make the cruise.

It ended up being a very, very special holiday. I was able to keep my mind off the operation and the cancer and just enjoy watching and being part of the fun. I listened to my inner child and went about having fun and living in the moment. My boys were relaxed about my illness because I was able to relax. They also saw their Grandmother doing well after her mastectomy so they had reason to be optimistic about me.

Speaking to friends who have been diagnosed with cancer I know I was a little unusual in this respect. Most people just want it OUT and can't wait to get the process started so it can finish sooner. But the extra time also allowed me to get a lot of extra opinions and decide on a full mastectomy rather than a lumpectomy or only having one breast removed. I had time to plan my long-term outcome and how I wanted to look and feel once the whole process was over.

MY PLAN

It was important for me to feel that I had some sort of control over everything that was happening to me during the whole process. So, I made plans and set goals. It started with making sure lots of family and friends came to visit me in hospital so the time went quickly. I was a little optimistic having family visit the night of my mastectomy and I may not have been the best company for them, but it felt awesome having everyone there.

The second night was New Year's Eve and visitors were supposed to leave by 8pm. But Anthony and I hadn't been apart on New Year's Eve in 31 years and he wasn't about to break that tradition. He came back to a locked-up hospital at 10pm and the nurses were so impressed seeing him with flowers and chocolates that they let him in. Never would I have imagined shuffling down the hospital halls in that state at the age of 50. But it was so special that my best friend was there with me.

The next part of the plan was to get through another three operations (maybe four) and 12 weeks of weekly Chemo. After that, I had other treatments every three weeks but that wasn't such an effort. During all of this my goal was to pick the kids up from school if I was able, cook dinner if I was able and get an A+ in Netflix. I had slowed down all of my work and I even went through and harshly unsubscribed from everything to make sure my email didn't get out of control.

The next 12 weeks were quite social for me. Friends would drive the kids to school, family would drop in for a cup of tea and always bring homecooked meals. Lots of people called and I had time for long and cherished chats with special people in my life. I knew I needed to let everyone know about my diagnosis and I couldn't get to everyone by calling them so I posted my story on Facebook. Part of that post included thank you's and gratitude, plus one request. I wrote:

Dear friends. I am hesitant to put this on FB as I am not trying to get attention or sympathy. But I have not been able to keep up on all your PMs which I am so grateful for. So here is the update. My mastectomy went well. Today I went in for a quick day surgery and had a portacath put in so I can start Chemo next week. I will have weekly injections of Taxol for 12 weeks and Herceptin every 3 weeks for 12-months. Additionally I have lots of natural things I am doing to stay healthy. So there is no need to send me lots and lots of product ideas as I feel I am really on the right track. I have some incredible experts whom I am working with. I am very grateful for all the people who have helped me thus far and continue to support me. I love all your messages and appreciate all my friends. I understand that some people disagree with my choices and I will be happy to debate them in 12 months' time. But just not yet. Thanks everyone for your incredible support. I look forward to partying with you in 2019.

This post got 450 comments and over 600 likes. Only two people disagreed with my decision to go through chemo. If others disagreed, they didn't burden me with their beliefs which I was immensely grateful for. I realise that some people disagree with chemo but I truly believe that most of those people would have a tough time rejecting it if put in my position.

My chemo nurses were truly amazing, lovely people. I was fortunate to have a different friend take me to each of my 12 weekly sessions which gave me four hours of quality time with each special friend. I was able to keep walking for exercise during this time but I did get slower and slower. I got "HelloFresh" pre-shopped meals delivered so I didn't have to get to the supermarket but I was able to cook great nutritious food for my family.

I made it my mission to raise money for the Australian Cancer Council and families in need. It became clear to me that there were people in our community who were given their cancer diagnosis and suddenly found themselves unable to work and support their families. For single-parent families, this is even more challenging and stressful. This was the catalyst for me raising money for the Australian Cancer Council who provide financial assistance for families in need.

This is now one of my chosen charities for life. People have asked me, "Why give to the Cancer Council for research when more and more people are getting cancer, it doesn't seem like the charities are effective?"

My response is that in 2005, women would have died with my type of cancer but due to incredible research and development, clearing my type of cancer now has a significant success rate. It's due to non-profits like the Australian Cancer Council that these discoveries are made and it's up to *us* to make sure their research can continue.

At this time, I will be donating $2 from every printed version of this book to the Australian Cancer Council and putting on fundraising events.

On the 21st of February, I asked my hairdresser to give me an interim short haircut so I knew what I would be growing it back to once my hair started growing again. After she chopped it off, I donated my ponytail to a charity that made wigs for children going through illness. I also got my eyebrows tattooed while I still had them so the tattoo artist could follow my natural eyebrow line.

My hair began falling out after chemo number six. It was disconcerting and scary when handfuls of hair started falling out. I went to a free, feel-good event called "Look Good – Feel Better" which was an incredible organization for helping women going through treatment. The ladies were all survivors and they gave massive amounts of free makeup and skin care and showed us how to look great even without hair.

Other ladies there were also in the early stages of losing their hair but one lady who was much younger than me and had babies had lost her hair and was the model for trying on wigs. I was so inspired by her strength.

In the 12 months from my diagnosis, I only cried 4 times. These were only short sessions and usually occurred when I was driving. I really didn't want to waste time worrying about what might happen until it happened. I knew I had life insurance and that was the only precaution I could think about.

One of the days I did cry was when my wonderful friend Jackie flew up to spend the day with me. Our first job was to get my makeup done at Myer and then get my head shaved. My hair had been falling out so quickly that it was time to remove what was left and then buy a wig. I was fine getting my head shaved but when I went to pay, the hairdresser said it was free. That's when I cried for a moment. After that it was time to go to the wig shop and have some fun. I must admit that I only wore my wig 4 times as I preferred scarves but it was an important gesture in my journey and was definitely part of my recovery plan and taking control of some areas of my life. A number of friends gave me beautiful, multicoloured scarves and one talented friend even made me a beautiful blue silk turban "to match my eyes".

The only saving grace in having a shaved head was that people instantly knew I was going through treatment and seemed to be nicer to me. Plus, my husband has a shaved head so we looked like twins. My hair grew back "shock-white" which was quite interesting but as it grew longer it got very curly and just looked grey. I made the decision that I would not be grey in my 50s so I began colouring it. At some stage, I may get it straightened and maybe even hair extensions to speed up the process. My tattooed eyebrows continue to be a feature. I like them and I may even continue to get them touched up.

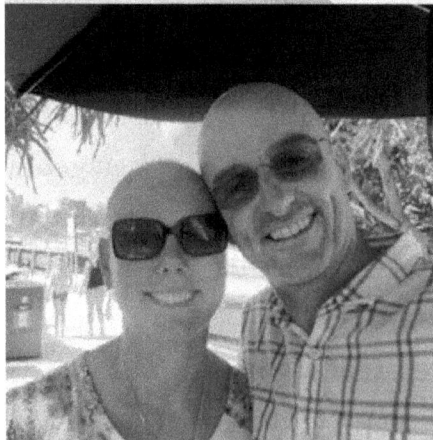

On a private note, I have to go back to the tattoo artist to get my new nipples. Did I mention the originals had to go because the cancer was too close to save them? This was not as emotional as I would have predicted because my surgeon wants to rebuild some when I go in to get my portacath out. Add that to 3D tattoos and it becomes hard to tell the difference. I'm grateful for the fact that I now have young, perky boobs like I did when I was in my twenties. The scars are becoming unnoticeable.

The chemo brought on menopause and hot flushes right in the middle of Summer. Sleeping through the night was impossible because I would wake up seven or more times a night as my body heated up. On top of that, the Steroids helped me put on 8kg of unwanted weight that put me in the "obese" category at 85kg.

But despite my weight gain and chemo symptoms, I still had enough energy to do fun things with the family every weekend. We were able to take weekends away with the kids and I started volunteering at Park Run. I was taken to all the Commonwealth Games events in a wheelchair but I was treated like a princess. I felt like I was coping with everything that was happening to me so I was able to smile and joke and not feel the need to think about my future too much. I stuck to my values and let people help me if they offered.

My body image had to change after the mastectomy. I had expanders put in after my breast tissue was removed which came with remote controls. The technology allows you to inflate the expanders over a number of weeks because there are compressed air canisters inside and the remotes release a small amount of air into the bladders. I would joke with my husband and ask him to "blow up my boobs".

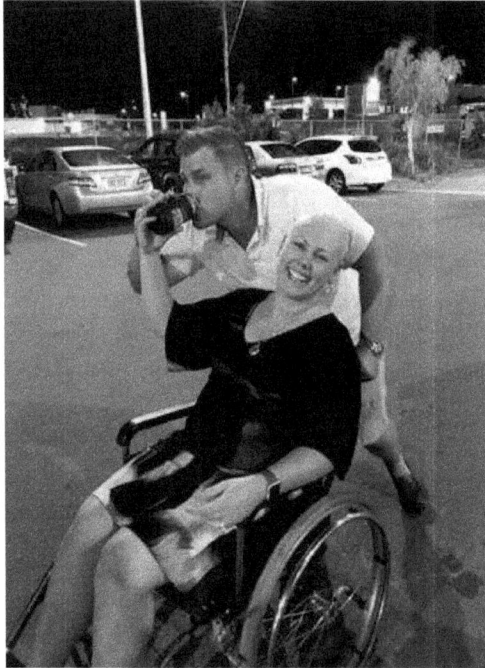

In April, I got on a plane and realized going through security that the compressed air canisters were what was setting off the scanners. I let the workers believe their equipment was faulty.

I read or listened to a book every week (mostly fiction) and I finished a whole lot of online courses that I had signed up for and never completed. It felt good to get these things accomplished.

In June, I went back to the coaching course I started in November and I was able to coach all my pro-bono clients and earn my certification in Advanced Business Coaching.

My Facebook post then read:

"These photos were taken 8 months apart. We never know what life is going to throw at us. Which makes it so important to enjoy every moment, whilst never forgetting to plan for our future. My advice to you is "Make every moment count! Don't waste time living by rules that don't serve you. Love who you are and make the world a better place because you are in it."

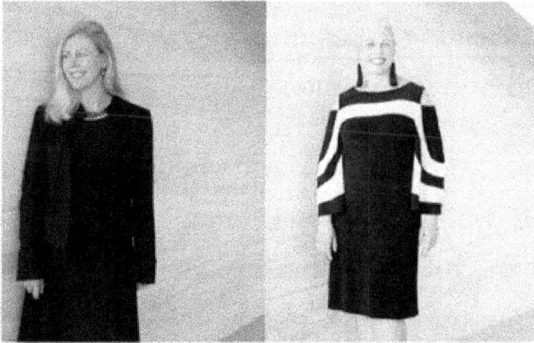

These photos were taken 8 months apart. We never know what life is going to throw at us, which makes it so important to enjoy every moment, whilst never forgetting to plan for our future. My advice to you is "Make every moment count! Don't waste time living by rules that don't serve you. Love who you are are and make the world a better place because you are in it."

MY RECOMMENDATIONS TO NEWLY DIAGNOSED CANCER PATIENTS

- Don't be fearful. Decide on a plan of action that suits your illness and your desired outcome and make it work for you. Do as much research as you need to feel satisfied with your plan and then request that friends and family support you in your chosen plan.

- Have a vision for your future that makes you so excited and contributes in your own way to society. Use this future vision of you as an affirmation for your healing. Help your body by doing affirmations regularly.

- Be Patient. It's natural to want to get back to your old levels of energy but give your body time and be kind to yourself. Healing takes time and you need to be nice to yourself in the meantime.

- If possible, set aside two hours per day for self-care. This could be walks, massages, meditation, floats, saunas, yoga, gym, bike, swimming, horse riding, journaling or anything that helps you manage stress and keep you healthy. It sounds like a lot of time a day but it's not just exercise – it's also time for you to regenerate.

- Stay emotionally strong by having positive people around you and later by helping others.

MY TIPS FOR MANAGING WORK AND BUSINESS DURING TREATMENT

- Talk to survivors to get a realistic idea of what your energy levels will be during and after treatment.

- Cut back all non-income producing activities at work or business.

- Delegate jobs that are time-sensitive as you cannot guarantee you will feel up to it.

- Delay new projects until you're feeling well enough.

- Where possible, prepay bills or set early reminders so you don't run out of stock, electricity or other important resources.

- Accept help from friends and family, especially chores at home, driving children around, and food preparation.

- Decide if it's appropriate to tell staff and customers what you are doing and how it will affect them. You will probably find that everyone is very accommodating and leave you alone or help you more.

- Decide if you need to sack your bottom 20% of customers who cause you more work than your top profitable customers.

- Work from home more and use technology for meetings rather than traveling.

- Check your insurances – do any of them provide for you being out of action for a period of time or payout based on your written diagnosis?

"Find the gift from your illness and use your gift to help others."

– Megan Wolfenden

PART TWO

NEXT STEPS –
BUILD STRENGTH

In this section, you'll get strategies you can use to begin to rebuild your physical, mental and financial self. Healing takes time and patience. It's important to heal all areas of your life, set goals and start achieving new and exciting successes.

Each small accomplishment will build on the previous ones and within no time at all you can get your life back on track and be your best self. Take any of the topics in this chapter and implement them into your daily or weekly habits. Remember to think BIG and positively impact as many people as you can. This can be your legacy.

SELF CARE

I have put this as the top practise in the list because all the survivors I have spoken said that before they got sick, self-care wasn't enough of a priority. Parents would often put the needs of their children way before self-care. Entrepreneurs would put their work before prioritising self-care. Everyone seems to have priorities in their lives that go before their own health.

When I talk about self-care, it covers everything from eating well, sleeping well, getting enough exercise, getting enough downtime, massage, sauna, floats, team sports, getting back to nature, managing stress, taking re-energising vacations, meditation, social engagements and even community involvement. Most people have some of these things scheduled into their week but still don't put enough time or emphasis on doing more of these things each day. It does take time but it's time well spent.

The Dalai Lama once said what surprises him most about humanity is, "Man. Because he sacrifices his health in order to make money. Then he sacrifices his money to recuperate his health. And then he is so anxious about the future that he does not enjoy the present; the result being that he does not live in the present or the future; he lives as if he is never going to die, and then dies having never really lived."

Let's take self-care a step further and add parenting ourselves. This means allowing ourselves to be human, make mistakes and not be perfect. Having said that, it also means paying our bills on time, having a budget and planning for our financial future. This might sound like a lot but if you are a parent, you're already thinking about these things for your children, so make sure you are giving yourself that same gift. It also means saying no to toxic relationships, unhealthy excesses in your life and behaviours that don't set you up for success.

- Journal 4 ways you are going to improve your own self-care:

_____

_____

_____

_____

EMOTIONAL RECOVERY

There will be times when you want to look back and ask, "Why Me?" While some reflection on your past lifestyle and self-care is important, it's also important to realize that constantly looking back is not helpful. You may have a spiritual belief that helps you understand what has happened to you but most people work up to the point of saying, "This happened and now I am going to make the most of my lessons learnt and look forward to, and work towards, a better tomorrow."

You may need a coach or counsellor or therapist to help you move through your stages of grief or anxiety. Up to one-fifth of survivors are affected by PTSD. If you're feeling like you have symptoms of PTSD, seek immediate professional help. Remember that your family went through your illness with you. Your spouse or children may also need some outside support to get them through their feelings about your illness.

Your emotional recovery is as important as your physical recovery. Keeping a journal and writing your random thoughts throughout your treatment and recovery can be very therapeutic. Don't underestimate the importance of working through and coming to terms with your trauma.

- Journal 4 ways you are going to improve your Emotional Recovery:

_____

_____

_____

_____

YOU ARE ENOUGH!

It's so common to believe we're not enough. This is especially the case after treatment when you're not yet back to your physical or mental best. We get this crazy idea that we're not the best parent, spouse, sister, brother, daughter, son, friend, worker, leader, etc. We beat ourselves up and think of all the ways we're not good enough.

This feeling can stay with us forever unless we understand it's the little voice inside us that's not serving us. The truth is, if you brought a group of your friends together and were told to secretly analyse them, you would never think one of them was not enough. The same if we bought a group of co-workers or community associates together. Never would we say they were not good enough for whatever they were doing in their lives.

Our inner voice can be really harsh. Way harsher than we would ever be with our best friends. That inner voice can be especially damaging when we're run down and tired or when we have delayed hitting a milestone or worse, we've had someone else tell us we're no good.

Instead of listening to that inner voice, let your Inner Child shine through. A child can live in the moment without criticizing and see happiness in the little things.

To overcome this harsh inner voice, we must make a pact with ourselves to treat ourselves as we treat our best friends. We must be compassionate, caring, honest and forgiving. Always speak kindly to yourself and realize that beating yourself up is creating an unsuccessful environment and a self-fulfilling prophecy.

- Journal 4 ways you can prove to yourself you ARE enough:

_____

_____

_____

_____

MEDITATE

This word has a wide variety of methodologies associated with it. Because of this, it's easy to believe we don't know *how* to meditate and never even try. But the benefits of meditations are numerous. For starters, a simple breathing meditation can instantly calm a situation by making you feel more centred and giving healthy oxygen back to the whole body.

Other short-term effects of meditation can be clarity of mind, peacefulness to allow for sleep, or rejuvenation to allow someone to continue with their day. Long-term benefits of meditation include recovery from illness, less anxiety, self-awareness, joy, improved relationships, better ability to cope with stress and develop businesses, and an overall sense of vitality and health. It also helps with memory, learning, decision-making and creativity.

For someone new to meditation, I suggest guided meditations that relate to a particular outcome you want to achieve. Here are a few of my top suggestions of where to begin:

- If you're not sleeping well, try Bob Proctor's "Guided Sleep Meditation".

- If you're fearful or anxious, I suggest the "Let Go" Meditation on YouTube.

- If you're feeling like life is a struggle every day and things don't come easy to you, I suggest "Detachment From Overthinking" on YouTube.

As you become accustomed to meditating, I suggest classes to really develop your skills. There are many different kinds of meditation. Some for you to research are:

- Mindfulness Meditation

- Kundalini Yoga

- Zen Meditation

- Transcendental Meditation

- Guided Visualisation

- Vipassana Meditation

- Qigong

- Journal how you are going to incorporate meditation into your schedule. What meditation style is of interest to you?

_____

_____

_____

_____

UNDERSTAND YOUR PURPOSE

When we're faced with the possibility of dying from cancer, we definitely think about our contribution, our legacy and why we were put on this earth. Having this insight, and being able to objectively look at how we impact the people around us and how we can leave the earth a better place from our having lived, gives us clearer meaning in our lives.

Make sure you take the time to write out what you have learned and clarify your purpose. Most importantly, clarify what it is you want to accomplish for the remainder of your life. How are you going to make a difference and contribute? Contribution can be in the form of helping others, helping the environment, standing up for an important cause, creating works of art or literature or music, making people laugh or fostering education.

Have a *reason* for doing what you are doing.

- What would you like to accomplish or contribute to society?

_____

_____

_____

_____

CONFIDENCE

Having confidence means believing in yourself and your abilities. It means not criticising yourself or always believing that someone else does a better job at something than you do. It's about accepting and embracing your differences and uniqueness and being content with who you are. When you're in a situation you feel confident and relaxed in, how do you act, speak and stand? Intentionally practise using those traits when you're in situations that you feel less confident in and in time these situations will also become comfortable.

If you're feeling anxious about an upcoming meeting or situation, sit down with a pen and paper and write out your ultimate outcome. What is it you want to achieve at this encounter? Think of your best-case scenario. Then role play in your mind how you could make it happen. Plan your outfit and commute so you are on time, and rehearse the dialogue that gets you your outcome. The more detail you can describe in advance, the better prepared you will be. Having preparation will take some anxiety away.

Once you arrive at the event, take time to breathe, smile, run through your plan and jump in. The more you put yourself into this position to grow, the quicker you will feel confident and accomplished.

Also, let yourself off the hook if you don't get your preferred outcome. Talk to yourself like you are your own best friend.

To really build confidence, join Toastmasters and learn the art of presenting. Any learning environment like this will improve your confidence and set you up for success.

- Journal 4 ways to increase your confidence:

_____

_____

_____

_____

HAVE FUN

Instead of thinking there will be a magic destination in our future where we're always happy and having fun, realise that the time to have fun is right NOW. Living in the moment, enjoying a joke, laughing at something silly that happened or recognising that a situation is special lets you feel happiness in the moment. And these moments add up to great times. Seeing this and taking note of these times will help you feel grateful and happy for longer. Making smiling, fun and happiness a habit creates a sense of wellbeing and reduces stress. Make sure that you seek out fun by scheduling fun, interesting and enjoyable events into your life.

- Journal 4 ways you can add fun into your calendar:

_____

_____

DON'T COMPARE

There will always be people out there doing something more exciting than you perceive you're doing, or having more "luck" than you perceive you're having, or traveling to exotic places you want to go to or buying things you admire. This list goes on and on.

You can strive to be, do or have any of these things but do it on *your* terms. Be the best version of yourself, plan who it is you want to be, work hard and achieve all the things you want to achieve. But never think someone else is better just because they are doing, being or having something you want.

When we assess someone else based on the few things we know about them and then compare ourselves to them, we're forgetting they are a whole person with their own experiences, challenges, illnesses or other issues that we may not know about. Never wish you were someone else because you wouldn't want to take on someone else's journey. You were built for YOUR journey and you are becoming the best version of YOU.

If you continue to compare yourself to others, work out why this is important to you. Are you feeling insecure in some areas of your life and therefore letting your self-esteem get affected? Are you worried about things in your life and believe that no one else has those same issues? When you understand why you are comparing yourself to others you can work out how to overcome the issue and find ways to stop this behaviour. Focusing on why you are YOU and why you are unique will be far more productive and helpful to you.

- Journal areas of your life where you don't give yourself enough credit:

_____

_____

_____

_____

HAPPINESS

When we're focused on happiness and joy, we cannot be stressed. Now that you're recovering from cancer, think about life as a gift and that every moment is to be enjoyed. To change your state of mind, listen, sing or dance to music, get creative, look at beautiful art, get into nature or play with a child. It's important to focus on "looking at the bright side" of situations.

You have a choice. You can sit in the corner and be upset about how things have turned out or you can project forward knowing you are working on making the best of every situation. Being "happy for no reason" improves your hormones, improves body function and makes you fun to be around.

I have clients who have come to me because there were looking for a Happiness Coach. To get them excited about life again, I have a lot of tools and techniques that all contribute towards this goal. But the first two things we work on are having short-term goals they can accomplish and feel great about and working towards some rewards in their life that make their daily routines feel like they're moving in the right direction. The daily act of working ON happiness really gets results.

Please note if you have symptoms of depression, seek immediate help from a professional or call Beyond Blue https://www.beyondblue.org.au

If you love the idea of working with a Happiness Coach, contact me through www.meganwolfenden.com

- Journal 4 things that make you feel happy and you need more of in your life:

_____

_____

_____

_____

FIND YOUR COMMUNITY

Finding a group of people who make you feel appreciated can have a huge positive impact on your life and how you feel about yourself. Humans need to belong to something or have a cause that drives them and community groups fulfil that human need. Seek out organizations that appeal to your values. Meetup groups are popping up everywhere, each with different goals and reasons for meeting. Try new groups until you find some that resonate with you. Some examples are:

- Charity groups e.g. Lions Club, Rotary

- Investing groups e.g. property or crypto

- Educational groups e.g. languages, web design, home vegetable gardening

- Mixers e.g. book clubs, traveling groups, personal development groups

- Creative groups e.g. scrapbooking, knitting

- Religious e.g. churches, bible studies

- Journal where you want to meet new people or what new hobby you want to try:

_____

_____

_____

_____

ACCEPT IMPERFECTION

No one is perfect but for some reason most of us believe that other people have fewer imperfections than we do. We need to look at what we're good at and magnify this, understand where we need improvement, work on that over time and let go of areas where we don't need to be better.

Criticism of our flaws does not serve us. It simply upsets us and hold us back from achieving success. Accept that you're not meant to be perfect and you will be a life-long learner until the day you leave this earth. The *journey* is what's important because we keep moving the destination. If we hit the destination and had nothing more the strive for, we would go nowhere and do nothing. Make improvements all the time and rejoice in your journey of improvement.

- What areas of your life do you need to stop beating yourself up over?

_____

_____

_____

_____

ROUTINE – MANAGE YOUR TIME

Having control over your time helps you get more done and gives you a feeling of accomplishment. Know the most important things you need to get done each week by writing a list. Transfer that list to your daily calendar or diary and make a pact with yourself to work on those important things first. This can be difficult at first but turn it into a habit by putting in conscious effort for 30 days. By the end of that time, you'll see how much you got done, how good it feels and you'll want to keep going.

Staying organized means you get to appointments on time and without stress, you get the important things done and you get your bills paid on time without late fees.

The next stage is to make a list of important goals you want to achieve. Then create an action item for each of these goals. Put these action items in your daily calendar and start achieving each day.

To help you get started, grab your free goal setting worksheet here: https://meganwolfenden.com/goals

- Journal 4 goals you want to achieve and how you can get more organised to achieve them:

_____

_____

_____

_____

RESILIENCE

Resilience is the ability to bounce back when something doesn't go your way. Some people naturally have this trait. Others have to work at it. If you have to work at it, understand that you can plan how you want to react to a situation. To build resilience if something goes wrong, ask yourself, "How can I learn from this?" "Who can help me?" and "Can I change something I am doing to make things better?" Ask the perspective of a good friend and see if they see a situation in a different light. Read books where people have overcome adversity and learn from their methods.

You can have two different perspectives for the same situation. For example, if you have a small car accident where no one is hurt you can

a) be upset that the incident is going to cost you time and money to fix, or

b) be happy that no one was hurt and the cars are fixable.

Having the ability to see both perspectives can help you decide which scenario you are going to focus on. Taking the optimistic view helps you build resilience.

- Journal times in your life when you have been resilient:

_____

_____

_____

_____

SLOW IT DOWN - DON'T BE BUSY

Being "busy" can feel stressful and stop us achieving large tasks because we favour getting smaller things ticked off our to-do list. We can even start to resent social engagements because they just look like more to do on our list. When every hour of our day feels scheduled and accounted for, our adrenaline can spike and we can feel anxious. When this feeling continues over a prolonged time with lots of stress hormones released, we can get adrenal burnout.

Because we're trying to improve our health, not make it worse, it's so important to stop this busy cycle. Some of our tasks are important and MUST get done, but there is also a good portion that we can stop doing or delay to ensure we have time to enjoy life.

It's important to think about the benefit of doing something before we say yes to something. If we fear missing out, have a desire to please people or simply want to experience and accomplish a lot in a short time, it's easier to overcommit in advance than to think about our health and enjoying our relaxed, calm lives.

Take note of how you fill your days and then mindfully adjust your calendar. Start with necessities in your day like looking after your family and going to work, then add in important tasks like exercise, healthy eating, enjoyable social events and meditating. Eliminate time wasters like social media or unplanned screen time and television.

It's said that we overestimate what we can get done in a day and underestimate what we can get done in a year. So, use a calendar and plan out your important and fulfilling events. After that, only add important or rewarding tasks. Managing your time in a mindful way ensures the important things always get done and you can let go of the tasks that don't serve you or your family.

Small changes to your schedule can make a huge difference. Sticking to a schedule helps you be on time for appointments and chunk your time so you know what the most important thing is that needs to get done at any particular time. When you are clear about your goals and chunk them down into smaller, manageable tasks you can get a lot accomplished. Look out for ways you procrastinate and realize these things are time wasters that take time away from your fun and family events.

Another important aspect of slowing down is making sure your planning is done in the beginning. Planning ahead reduces mistakes and makes time feel like it's flowing at our pace, not at a speed beyond what we can handle. Being methodical makes the task more controlled and enjoyable.

Slowing down also relaxes the people around you. Rather

than seeing you always rush and get stressed over getting things done, they see you as controlled, methodical and accomplished.

- Journal times you can say "no" to requests. How can you slow down and enjoy each moment?

_____

_____

_____

_____

EXERCISE

Get moving! After surgery, chemo and radiation the body needs great blood flow. At the beginning of your recovery, this may mean small movements and just a little time and effort. As your body heals you need to increase your movement as much as possible and with your doctor's permission. If you have physiotherapy as part of your treatment, ensure that all recommended at-home exercises are completed to speed up recovery.

Respect and value your body. Get an expert to give you an exercise regime that suits your abilities and sets you on a path to daily improvement. Get outside in nature and breathe fresh air whenever possible. Set a plan to get back to your old "normal" and then go above and beyond your old self. We know the benefits of daily exercise but many people don't make it a daily priority because other commitments win our time. Find a form of exercise that interests you and feels right for your body.

Make finding your favourite exercise a game you set for yourself. Try different things out for a month or two each and work out your optimum workout plan. Trial different gyms and find a group class with people you find interesting. Find stretching classes, Pilates, hiking groups, road or mountain bike groups, dog walking groups, sailing clubs, surfing lessons, horse riding trails, rock climbing gyms, aqua aerobics pools etc. Don't stop until you find your niche and make it an important part of your life.

- What exercise would you like to try? What exercise schedule would work with your lifestyle?

_____

_____

_____

_____

FOOD AS FUEL

If, like me, you have put on a lot of weight from steroids during chemo, it's time to take action and get back to your pre-illness weight. While you're at it, why not go for a personal best? You need to make sure your attitude about food is healthy and will sustain a long and healthy life. Maybe some of the indulgences of your past must be cut right back or eliminated. You may need to investigate various philosophies out there and trial different plans to see what suits your body and your lifestyle.

Common post Cancer diets include:

- High Alkaline

- Keto

- Mediterranean

- Paleo

- Juice Fasting

- Intermittent Fasting

- Plant-based

Knowing what choices you have and why people do or don't like a particular strategy will make you better informed and allow you to decide what is right for you. The more education you get around nutrition the better. This is an ongoing and ever-changing area where experts do not agree on one stand-out theory which is why you need to make your own decision about your nutrition.

You are looking for a sustainable, balanced, long-term approach to the way you eat and socialize. Be realistic and get back to natural where possible.

- Journal the changes you would like to make with your food:

_____

_____

_____

_____

DEVELOP GRIT

Because you have come out of a tough illness, you know you already have grit. You stuck to your surgery, radiation or chemo or combo of those and you made it through. Always remember how strong you are and how much grit you really do have. If you think of grit as hard work and persistence, then you KNOW you have it. And you have what it takes to not only get back on your feet but to get further than you dreamed, and really live your best life.

Grit is a great predictor of success, so you are already part of the way there. Make sure you set HUGE long-term goals that are really going to make a difference in the world – because if you can beat cancer you can do anything! You have proven you have courage and the ability to bounce back from adversity. This resilience together with a drive to live your best life will ensure you leave a legacy. Use your grit to achieve amazing goals.

- Journal times you have shown grit and how you felt when you stuck with something:

_____

_____

_____

_____

GRATITUDE JOURNALING

I've found having gratitude puts life into perspective for me. This is an easy practise that doesn't have to take hours out of your day. Put a beautiful journal beside your bed and before retiring simply write five things you were grateful for that day. More than five if you're on a roll.

Being thankful improves your physical and mental health. If you are feeling angry about a person or situation, change your perspective by asking what it is about the situation you can be grateful for. This reduces the toxic and angry feeling you have towards a situation or person and allows you to work on the solution.

Noticing the great things in your life makes you feel happier and creates space for more incredible things to appear in your life.

- Journal 4 things you feel gratitude for today:

_____

_____

_____

_____

MAKE SLEEP A PRIORITY

Restful, continuous, regular sleep is so important for improving health. In our society, we don't value sleep as much as we value accomplishment. However, without adequate sleep our achievements are limited to our body's ability to focus and produce exceptional results. Starting with a base of excellent sleep is imperative for good physical and mental health.

Stress is one of the major disruptors to sleep. Practises mentioned in this chapter can assist with reducing stress before sleep, like meditation, writing in a gratitude journal, drinking adequate water throughout the day and exercise. It's also important to:

- Make sure your bedroom is dark and well ventilated

- Go to bed at the same time each night (preferably before midnight)

- Limit alcohol consumption

- Avoid napping for too long during the day

- How much sleep do you think you need? What steps can you take to make sure you get enough sleep each night?

_____

_____

_____

_____

UNDERSTAND STRESS

As mentioned earlier, stress can severely affect our health and wellbeing. A body that is constantly under stress is putting the immune system under pressure, and when you're recovering from cancer that's the last thing you want. We all have stressors in our lives but it is the way we *manage* stress that affects our health.

Some level of worry is avoidable. Of course, there are

times in our lives, like being diagnosed with cancer, when it can be very difficult to manage our stress. First, it is important to document what you are stressed about. Thinking about each stressor, ask yourself what steps you can take to alleviate the stress and schedule in when you can take those steps. Also, assess your worst-case scenario and see if the reality is not as bad as it seems. Often when we think about the worst-case, we get relief that we have options and can manage a situation better than we thought.

Lastly, realise that if you're worrying about things that have not actually happened yet, your concern is a waste of time and energy. Things may not play out as you imagine they might. Don't attract what you don't want by focusing on the wrong things. Focus on what you DO want.

If you're worried about expectations of others then assess if that is a worthwhile emotion. Do you or someone close to you have unrealistic expectations that you need to address?

- Journal 4 strategies you can use to reduce your stress levels:

_____

_____

_____

_____

CONTRIBUTION

When we help others, we put our own issues into perspective and often realize that we'll be fine and we are great just the way we are. We see others who have been dealt a different hand to us and they cope with far more adversity with strength and grace. Contribution can come in the form of money or time, expertise, donating resources or skills. We get a feeling of being needed and belonging when we give time to help others. It's a great stress reliever.

Every society relies on volunteers to get things done. Volunteers help stitch a community together. Involving the whole family in an event teaches children many life lessons and keeps a family bound with common-good ties.

Having been through an illness yourself, you know the value of a meal being dropped off or someone offering to take the kids to school for you. Those people paid it forward and now it's your turn to reciprocate or pay it forward to other families in need. Your life experiences are valuable to those families and you'll feel their gratitude when you help.

- How can you help out in your community?

_____

_____

_____

VALUE WHO YOU ARE, NOT WHAT YOU DO

We give ourselves titles and then we evaluate ourselves based on those titles. For example, you might identify as a Mum, wife, business person and sister. When the kids move out, our role as Mum changes and less time is given to this role. When we have little ones, we assess how GOOD a Mum we are and then when the role changes, we feel a part of ourselves is lost.

There is more value in recognising *who we are* than what we do. Who are you outside of the roles you play and how do you want people to think of you? Some examples include:

- A caring friend

- A generous listener

- A great person to go to for advice

- Someone who laughs a lot

- A lover of nature

- A great team player

- Well-read

- A great person to have a conversation with

- A loving soul

Think of yourself as having a set of character traits that make you the exceptional person you are, rather than the roles you fulfil at a particular time in your life. That way, as your life circumstances change, you still have your identity based on your character and therefore maintain your self-esteem.

- Journal a list of your personal attributes:

_____

_____

_____

_____

LEARN FROM THE PAST
AND LEAVE IT BEHIND

After diagnosis, it's natural to look back over your life and try and work out what you did wrong. Did I eat the wrong food? Spend too long on my phone? Drink too much? Have too much electromagnetic charge in the house? Not wash my fruit properly? Too much sugar? What other influences caused my cancer? This type of thinking, while natural, is not helpful to keep dwelling on.

I believe my cancer came on because of the way I dealt

with stress. Everyone has stress in their lives. Some people a lot more than others. Stressors and life difficulties are not something that should be compared to anyone else. We often justify and compare our problems with other people's problems but this isn't helpful. Having gratitude for your situation is very important and can reduce your stress.

In my case, I was going through some tough business problems in the two years before I got Cancer. I was not exercising and finding ways to manage stress, so I am convinced that holding in that stress was a huge contributor to getting cancer. This means that by looking back and working that out I can now make changes that will help me stay healthier in the future.

- What can you learn from your past and how will you use this moving forward?

_____

_____

_____

_____

SILVER LINING

It's amazing to me how people can always find a silver lining in a situation, even if it seems like the worst possible situation. In my case for example, I know I caught the cancer early and all of my treatment is more an insurance policy than a necessity.

As I write this, I'm visiting my friend whose 20-year-old son just tried to commit suicide this morning. He's in hospital right now and will be physically fine. But he will have a long rehab journey. The silver lining that my friend was able to see was a) he lived and b) he's in the right place and ready to make rehab work. He may have hit rock bottom but he can now work on getting better and be in a better place than he was a year ago.

How fabulous that we have the ability to see the silver lining in life.

I'm not saying we cannot dwell in our situation and let ourselves worry for a bit – that's natural. But to get over it and on with it quickly is so important for us to be able to get back to living our best life.

With every major life-lesson, we have to ability to grow and we become better humans afterwards.

- What is your silver lining?

_____

_____

_____

_____

"Cancer was the best, worst thing that has ever happened to me."

- Amy Kinnane

PART THREE

INTERVIEWS WITH FLOURISHING CANCER SURVIVORS

I had the pleasure of interviewing five amazing humans and hearing their courageous stories of how they recovered and flourished after their treatment. These inspiring people will give you hope and ideas for living your best life after cancer.

AMY KINNANE

Amy Kinnane lives on the Gold Coast of Australia with her husband and two young children. Since her treatment, Amy has gone on to become a role model for survivors by competing in Triathlons and getting her story out to the world via her blog and speaking engagements.

1. When you are introduced on stage, what is the most important thing you want people to know about you?

Amy Kinnane (AKA me) is a hilarious and extremely attractive 38-year-old Mother of two and Wife of one, living in sunny Australia. At the age of 36, she was diagnosed with Stage 4B Hodgkin's Lymphoma, just after her son's second birthday and eight weeks after her daughter was born. With her family by her side and friends cheering her on, Amy shares her entertaining version of events through treatment and remission as well as all the tears, fears and triumphs. This is her story, her world with kids, cancer and what life is really like after the Big C – Uncut and Uncensored.

2. What is your short cancer story?

December 3rd 2016, it was freakn' hot and I was away

on holidays with my family including my husband, kids and my parents. My little girl was eight weeks old and our little boy was two, so after six hours of packing the car for a two-day trip, we were on our way. We spent the next morning at the beach swimming, and by lunchtime we headed up to the apartment to put the kids down for a nap. We decided to crack open a few bev's as I hadn't had a drink since before I was pregnant and I was looking forward to a bit of normality. Anthony handed me a beer and I took a few sips. After about two minutes I had excruciating pain in my chest, my arms and my back, and it felt like a sledgehammer had hit me in the boobs. As my husband was trying to see if I was okay, he noticed I had a lump protruding out of my chest. At this stage the Panadol I had taken started to kick in and we decided, as mum and dad were there, I would go to the doctor to have a check-up. After several phone calls, no one could fit us in and the "At Home Doctors" didn't come out for chest pain. So (FML) I'm now off to the bloody hospital! We pack Indie's baby stuff up and Mum and Dad look after Kai. We say we will be back in a few hours and off we go to Emergency.

When we arrive at hospital, I go to the triage and by this time I'm feeling a bit stupid because I am feeling perfectly fine. I show them my chest lump like a freak and they send me off for some tests. Two hours later the doctor comes back and says after Googling my symptoms he has found some cases where alcohol reaction was caused by Hodgkin's

Lymphoma and so I am pushed off for a CT scan. He tells me I have a 1 in 4 million chance that this is it. I'm still not overly worried...and we wait.

There is now a storm outside, the wind is howling and Indie is sleeping in my husband's arms. It's 9pm and I'm freakn' starving. Finally, the doctor comes back and I'm excited to get going back to our holiday... He enters the room with a chair and closes the paper thin curtain ... "We have found what we didn't want to find...You have Cancer, and it's not good"... F**K!!!.... And the world goes silent.

What followed was seven long months of fortnightly chemotherapy, bone pain, sickness, hair loss and a massive emotional rollercoaster. But finally – remission. All whilst being a mother, wife, daughter and friend through the hardest and most life-challenging part of my life.

3. When you were first diagnosed, how was your mental health and what did you do to keep going?

This is a hard question for two reasons:

1) Because it's difficult to describe a mental state of mind on a general basis unless you use standard words like happy, sad, crazy or mad – that ain't me.

2) Because being diagnosed with cancer isn't just an instant reaction, it's a long, drawn-out emotional rollercoaster that

makes you delve into parts of yourself that you didn't even know existed. If I have to try to explain it in a few words, I would say PURE. UNIMAGINABLE. FEAR. The words "you have cancer" are instant and life-altering but the reaction and how you handle it always takes you by surprise. It's so different from what you would expect. You think you know yourself so well but in those vulnerable, twisted moments, your response is just so raw.

I went numb for the first two weeks before I was properly diagnosed. After that I was given a treatment plan and once I had some kind of structure, I just got into fight mode. I just put on my amour and I went into battle, not thinking a lot about what it actually was I was doing. I didn't feel much until the big guns were drawn like the imminent scans, the times when I was stripped down and put onto cold machinery and I held my breath, constantly scanning for emotions on the faces of the doctors who held my results and my life in their hands. The emotions I felt the most are the ones of the people around me, my parents, my husband, my kids and I felt a lot of guilt. I think if there was one emotion that I felt the most I would say it was guilt and I still do to this day.

How I kept going was acting like my life was a series of tasks; I broke it down into moments in time, minutes, seconds and weeks to the dreaded chemo room and then I would transform back into Mum for my children. I cooked dinner,

I cuddled them, I loved them and then I cried in the arms of my husband, on the bathroom floor, in the shower once they were asleep in their beds. I just had to fight and lean on my family to get me through.

4. What business/work were you doing before you got sick and how was this affected?

I am in recruitment and I was actually on maternity leave when was diagnosed. I went back for a few days here and there during treatment however due to my low immune system and as the chemotherapy built up, I got too sick to go back. After treatment, my husband and I decided to sell our house in Brisbane and move to the Gold Coast where my best friend and family live. I was lucky enough get a job with Maven Dental Group who have been incredibly supportive in my transition back into the working world.

5. Was there a financial burden on you and your family when you got sick? Did you need to keep working?

I couldn't go back to my job as was planned after my maternity leave was over and I had to resign. My husband had just started a new job and therefore had no holidays and had to use his long service leave money from his previous company that we had been saving to one day build our dream house. We were so lucky we even had that option and were able to have some form of money coming in to pay our mortgage. That ran out very quickly and from then on, our main concern was keeping everything as normal and in routine as possible for our children. It was incredibly difficult and just another blow to our lives while trying to deal with something that was so traumatic and out of our control.

6. During treatment, what did you do to keep optimistic?

I am a very outgoing and positive person but to be honest I had started mentally planning my funeral in the weeks after my treatment. This was because no one could answer me when I asked, "Am I going to die? How bad is it? How long do I have?" They were all answers that could only come with proper diagnosis, and that was entrapped in the waiting for results. Naturally, when you hear "cancer" and knowing how big my tumours were, I had to plan for the worst. I was just numb and in shock in those weeks. Once we got to the hospital one of the nurses said to me, "Hey, I have looked at your blood results and charts… don't start planning your funeral, you can come back from this."

That was the moment I changed my mindset because someone gave me a glimmer of hope, and that's all I needed. After that I was my bubbly self, cracking jokes and trying to make people laugh. I think I did that to try and alter the mood of people around me, as no one really knows what to say. Even the people you have known your entire life seem to have this weird shift in them. People don't know what to say, so I found comfort in making jokes about my bald head, my weight gain and the fact that I'd s**t myself. It definitely keeps you going.

I also believe that it's a mindset. If I was to finish chemo and then go and lie in a dark room, I think that would make me feel worse. Instead, I would make dinner, play with the kids and try to do normal things as much as I could. Having the kids really kept me going, and having a newborn doesn't stop just because your life has gone into a spiral.

7. How did you change your health routine once you were diagnosed?

My immune system is terrible now so the number of probiotics and vitamins I take has quadrupled. Also, Chemotherapy is a double-edged sword. All you want is for it to be over, yet when it is, you feel bare, vulnerable and scared because you feel unprotected. I think once I got out of the "Chemo bubble" I focused on anything I could do in my power to prevent it from coming back. If that means bathing in kale water, I'm doing it. Oh, I'm training for a triathlon! Yeah, whose idea was that?

8. After treatment, what parts of your life did you have to change or improve?

Everything. It's the best, worst thing that's ever happened to me. The world looks different, I see time differently, I see people differently and I see myself differently. If I could bottle what I have learned and pass it out as gifts, I would. Life is short and never be afraid of giving yourself everything you have ever wanted.

The night I was diagnosed we had to drive back to Brisbane at 1am. My husband, Indiana, and I stopped in at the house on the way to the hospital because I just wanted to have a shower in my own bathroom before I started whatever it was I was just about to start. When we were laying on the bed, all I remember thinking is "All I want to do is play with the kids, wash the dishes, do the laundry, watch TV..." It wasn't the big stuff I missed or desperately wanted, it was the basics, the small stuff, the stuff we take for granted. I will never forget that.

9. After treatment, how did your working/business life change?

I don't stress the small stuff. I don't stress about things. I don't worry about it and I work harder. I have a different fire driving me these days. I love going to work.

10. What are your top 5 recommendations for people going through treatment?

- Find someone who is going through treatment too. You need these people! Find support groups and use them as a sounding board and as support. I made a beautiful friend, Ashley, who was going through the same thing as me and also had an 8-week-old baby. Ashley and I spoke hourly via text and on the phone. She was my strength when I didn't have any and understood everything I was going through. We went through diagnosis, treatment and remission together. As much as my family and friends were there with me, I needed her because it was an unspoken connection and she got me out of some very dark places.

- Don't be disappointed when people you have known your whole life don't act in the way you want them to during and after treatment. I learned that everyone handles things in their own way. The most unexpected people will be by your side and others will turn their backs.

- Let go of the person you used to be and let yourself love the person you are now. Don't spend time trying to get your "old self back" because the "new you", although unknown, is something special.

- Give your marriage time to reset. I thought I would come out of chemo and conquer the world with everything going back to normal, but instead, it's been a long process of finding out about how trauma has affected me, my husband, our marriage and what life means to us now. I think the people by your bedside never really have the time to mentally accept what is happening and never really get to say how they are feeling. I mean, how do you tell someone you love, you are trying to protect, that you are scared they will die? Know when to stop and let yourself feel your emotions and when you and they are ready, let them tell you how they were feeling. It's all part of the healing process and necessary to move on in the same direction, together. It's normal to have to find each other again. Give yourself time to shine again.

11. What are your top 5 recommendations for people after treatment, who want to rebuild their physical, mental and financial health?

- Start Moving

- Set realistic goals

- Live outside your comfort zone

- Listen to your body

- Let the fire in your soul burn brighter than any fire around you

12. Any other comments?

We have been given a gift, use it as a second chance.

JOSIE TONG

Josie Tong has two daughters and comes from Sydney. She has a nursing background, is very successful in Network Marketing and is passionate about helping and training others. She wants to make a difference in the world by inspiring parents to work at home and spend more time with their children.

1. When you are introduced on stage, what is the most important thing you want people to know about you?

When I am introduced on stage, I want people to know that I quit a really, really good job because I was burnt out. I worked so much that I missed out on my kids' milestones, so now I am an advocate of women spending more time with their children while they are young. I can imagine that many parents, like myself, have a lot of regrets from missing out on their children's developmental milestones. I know that I missed out big time. I am very strong about that because I see a lot of children being taken to childcare at the age of 6 months or younger.

2. What is your short cancer story?

I worked as Director of Nursing for 17 years. It is a job that I loved and really enjoyed. However, due to the amount of work and pressure that I put on myself, I became a workaholic. My work became the centre of my life. I was working 50-70 hours a week for many years. When I was 46, I was burnt out from work and I quit my job with no plans or direction. I think that working that many hours and trying to be a Super Mum for my children took its toll. I had two children in my 40's. One was born when I was 40 years old and the second one was born when I was 43.

A year after I quit my job, I was diagnosed with breast cancer. I had surgery and five weeks of radiotherapy. This time of my life scared me more than ever. As I was being wheeled into the prep room before the operating theatre, I thought of my sister who died with breast cancer at a young age of 43. I prayed hard thinking of my very young kids. I wanted to see them walk down the aisle. I knew then that I would make it through and beat cancer. I knew then it was just a diagnosis and I could definitely recover from it.

3. When you were first diagnosed, how was your mental health and what did you do to keep going?

At the time I was diagnosed with breast cancer, I had a very busy full-on business with my international nursing agency. I was on the go all the time.

So, when the specialist told me that I had breast cancer and needed surgery, my mind was focused on "how can I beat it?" I wasn't depressed or anything. No time to feel sorry for myself. I was focused on getting myself better and being around for my kids.

What kept me going was my desire to live and see them walk down the aisle with their future husbands. I also had a big mission to accomplish, and that was to keep helping Nurses from the Philippines to work, study and live in Australia.

4. What business/work were you doing before you got sick and how was this affected?

After quitting my executive nursing job, I decided after a couple of months to start an international nursing agency. I was diagnosed after a huge batch of nurses arrived in Australia under my care. I didn't tell anyone about my condition. The only people who knew were my husband and my kids. I didn't want anyone to know. It took two years before I started sharing about it. My friends were in shock when they heard my news because they know how much I took care of my body - more than most of them.

I had an income stream coming from the agency and savings from my previous employment.

5. Was there a financial burden on you and your family when you got sick? Did you need to keep working?

I was fortunate that I had saved some money and had an

income stream from my nursing agency. I was working for myself so I had time-flexibility. My recovery was quite fast so I still managed to support the nurses that I brought over.

6. During treatment, what did you do to keep optimistic?

I think it is was my desire to be strong and healthy for my kids. I always believe in visualization and affirmation. So I always say to myself, "I am going to get through this. I am going to be healthy. I'm going to be there – and live 'til I'm 100." All that self-talk is important to me. When I lost my sister I was 37 years old. Fortunately, I caught my cancer early. The Mammogram I had was good timing because I hadn't had one for a while and I just thought it was about time to have one.

7. How did you change your health routine once you were diagnosed?

I don't remember any big changes in my health routine. I have mostly been a clean eater. Before my diagnosis, I didn't eat much junk food, nor had any soft drinks.

I had a regular walking and gym routine. So I didn't think I had to change much. What I included in my health regime were supplements, green juices and some meditation.

8. After treatment, what parts of your life did you have to change or improve?

I just remember driving to the hospital almost every day and in there were young and old people with beanies on, really looking terrible and I would think, "Oh My Gosh. I would not want anybody to go through this experience that I am going through." So at the time it was more about me encouraging my friends to get regular testing, by sharing my story that it was accidental that I went to get tested. Since then I encourage my friends to get tested and talk to their doctors. I became more aware and started sharing that with everyone I met.

9. After treatment, how did your working/business life change?

After treatment I stopped going overseas for business. Instead I started doing some consulting, which was good because it wasn't so stressful. I quite enjoyed it.

In 2009, however, I decided to set up my local nursing agency in Sydney. We converted our double garage into a home office and I was getting ready to launch the business locally in 2009. Two months before I was to launch in Sydney, a couple called me and asked if they could drop by. They started giving me a business presentation but I did not understand it. They started talking about pharmaceutical grade supplements. I made up my mind even before the presentation was over to join because I wanted to take the products that they were talking about.

This was a huge blessing for me.

When I made a decision to not launch my local agency and build my network marketing business instead, I went full-throttle. I grew my business very fast. I knew in my heart that I wanted to be home with my kids. I wanted to see them grow and be present. It was one of those decisions that has changed the direction of my life significantly.

As a single mum who is totally independent financially and able to raise my children single-handedly, it is a big testament to the benefits of a Network Marketing business.

10. What are your top recommendations for people going through treatment?

My sister just passed away in July this year from colon cancer and she opted not to have treatment. When I was visiting with her, I did a lot of reflection. Why do people have to go through this illness? This terrible disease? And I realized that if I was sitting down with someone younger and they were going through it, I would say to them "cancer is just cancer. There are so many people who beat cancer, you will be okay...you can beat this."

I believe in visualisation, so I would encourage them to see themselves much older, or 100 years old, and stay focused on the future. Sometimes I see that they are just so focused on how they are feeling right now but there is always hope.

And I would say to them this is a journey and there is hope at the end. Because they are going through what they are going through, they are going to learn a lot of lessons and this will be a stepping stone to the person they are going to become. From what I have seen with other people's journey and my journey, you become more health conscious and more aware. The lessons that you learn through your journey are stepping stones to finding the greater version of yourself.

Also, you are not alone. There are millions of people that are going through it. Sometimes you feel alone but there is a lot of help out there, so don't hesitate to reach out. You can find them in groups on Facebook or Google support groups and join them. Especially read other people's stories and find people you resonate with. That's what I would do.

Another thing is, it is more about "self-care". I know when I was working, I was working ALL the time. I was looking after everyone else. I was looking after my family and hardly thought of myself. I always put my health last. So now I believe it is so important. When you are on a plane, they say put your own oxygen mask on first. So put self-care first and make this a priority and keep reminding yourself of that.

11. Any other comments?

Megan, we talked about the financial aspect of getting sick. Having been an employee then being in business and then moving into Network Marketing I believe that Network Marketing is a lifesaver for those times in your life when you are in turmoil. This is because you work for yourself, not by yourself. In 2014 I had a divorce. We sold our home, had disruption and moved, and now we are settled. The cool thing about building a strong business in Network Marketing is if your life goes through two years of rollercoasters, you can still earn residual income. You are able to take time off to look after your kids or your own health without upsetting a boss or stopping your income. This is why I recommend building a business before you really need it.

It's great that someone like yourself who is going through the journey is putting thoughts and inspiration on paper and being a beacon for others going through it.

JESSICA MAINE

Jessica lives in Perth, Australia and is a single mother of four boys. She inspires church and community groups with her teachings on resilience and second chances. Her goal is to reduce depression and PTSD in cancer survivors around the world.

1. When you are introduced on stage, what is the most important thing you want people to know about you?

I want people to know that I am bold and courageous. I am a single mother of four very busy boys. We lost my husband to Melanoma in 2009 when my boys were six, five and the twins were three. One of my twins has a disability. I got breast cancer in 2013 but coped because of the incredible support of my parents, in-laws and wonderful community. My family import business was also a saviour because I could work part-time during my recovery. It was important to me to recover stronger than ever to continue looking after my wonderful family.

2. What is your short cancer story?

We were on a family holiday in Fiji when I noticed a lump in my breast. From Fiji, I booked an appointment with my GP for the day after we returned home. Within a few days I got my initial diagnosis. When I got back into my car I broke down and cried. I was so worried about what would happen to my kids if I was not around. My car was parked in a building that treats chemo and I noticed that there was a mature lady in the car next to me who was also crying. We smiled and wound down our windows. She had just found out about her recurring cancer so we stopped and chatted for a while.

Not having a husband at home to call and discuss my diagnosis with felt lonely. But my parents and in-laws jumped in and helped with kids, my appointments and logistics. I had a double mastectomy, radiation and chemotherapy. The year was crazy but I was determined to get better quickly. My goal was to not miss out on any functions at the kids' school. I only missed a couple of sports events.

3. When you were first diagnosed, how was your mental health and what did you do to keep going?

The first few months were such a whirlwind of appointments and operations that I don't remember having time to feel sorry for myself. When I was around the kids, I stayed positive and didn't talk about any pain or discomfort. We watched a lot of TV together. My mental health was good because I trusted that the doctors I had were the best available and they said I had a very good chance of being cancer-free at the end of my treatment. I believed that and just did as I was told. My kids were my motivation and if ever I felt down, I had a couple of friends who were cancer survivors and they would give me a pep talk.

4. What business/work were you doing before you got sick and how was this affected?

All my working life I have been the National Sales Director in our family business, selling awnings, shade sails and window dressings for commercial projects. My customer base is very loyal and when they heard of my cancer, they were very supportive. We brought on two new salespeople to look after my clients and grow the business and my brother took over my management role. I am very fortunate to have had the ability to stop work and get well without financial burden. In fact, it gave me time to think about what I wanted to do when I got better, and when I was able to work again I actually added a new division to our business and moved into artistic commercial lighting. This has given me more creative work which has been very rewarding. In fact, I have been given a number of industry awards for my work.

5. Was there a financial burden on you and your family when you got sick? Did you need to keep working?

No, I continued to get paid and I had health insurance through my company that covered a good portion of my costs. I did eat into my credit cards a bit as there were additional medical expenses. It worries me that there are a lot of single mothers out there who are not in as good a position as me. When I come across women in that situation, I give financial support now but my goal is to set up a foundation that helps single mums affected by cancer. Stress is such a contributor to bad health and I think financial stress is very real for too many people facing this difficult illness.

6. During treatment, what did you do to keep optimistic?

At my treatments each week I came across people who were terminal and were turning up to Chemo to keep them alive for longer. It was amazing to me how positive these people were. They laughed and listened to others' stories. They had plans of what they were going to do for the week or month ahead of them. When I met them it was impossible for me to be grumpy or feel sorry for myself. It did no good to be upset and in fact it was a waste of precious time to be upset. I listened to a lot of comedy on YouTube and podcasts and just kept laughing. I looked forward to every dinner as we would all be together and communicating and enjoying each other's company. My friends always made me laugh and took me to movies.

7. How did you change your health routine once you were diagnosed?

I had thought I was quite healthy before my diagnosis. However, I did have the occasional glass of wine or dessert or sugary treats. I cut out sugar altogether. I went on a Keto diet for 12 months and now do a mild version of low carbs. I will often have juice fasts for up to three days if I decide to go off low carb for a spell.

I do less vigorous exercise. I like to hike and walk for hours. Now I am better at meditating and taking time out for myself. I also take each child out separately to an outing of their choice so I have private time with each person.

8. After treatment, what parts of your life did you have to change or improve?

I had to work less hours so I had time to get family things organized. I also got a cleaner once a week. Each child had a night when they had to cook dinner – this was a fabulous change and meant that I could be working on homework with other kids when the dinner was getting made. I think I stopped sweating the small stuff after my treatment.

9. After treatment, how did your working/business life change?

I was more excited about my own creative part of the business. I think my illness gave me a chance to think about how I wanted to work and this change has given me renewed enthusiasm. I am fortunate to have the flexibility to be at a lot of the kids' extra-curricular events and I never want to change that.

10. What are your top 5 recommendations for people going through treatment?

Do a lot of research before your treatment to make sure you are happy with the process you are jumping into. Slow it down if you must. Check out your doctors and get second opinions. Once you have decided on the right treatment for you, jump in and get top marks for your participation. Ask friends and family not to second guess your chosen treatment path by offering other solutions. Only hang around positive people.

11. What are your top 5 recommendations for people after treatment, who want to rebuild their physical, mental and financial health?

Make sure you are doing work that makes you feel fulfilled. Don't waste time on a job you hate. If you are unhappy with your job, do lots and lots of job interviews as practise or if you have an idea and the ability to pursue it, build your own business. Work is an important part of who we are so do something that makes you proud. If you are stuck in a job you don't like or that does not pay enough, start a weekend business that can help you change careers in the future. It's never too late to take action.

12. Any other comments?

Cancer, if caught early, can be just a small part of your life story. Know that you can get past it and still do amazing things with your life. Think about the other people you can help and you will feel needed and valued. There is always someone worse off who needs your help.

ALEX LIBERMAN

Alex lives in Melbourne with his wife and two teenage boys

who are into sports and education. He is a User Experience Expert and says, "I'm a pragmatic person who values attitude, humility, empathy and growth. I strongly believe that the relationships we create and maintain define us not only as people but as businesses as well." At the time of writing, he is in treatment for recurrent bowel cancer and has found alternative therapies together with traditional therapies are working well and his body is in healing mode. He teaches optimism and humility and he loves teaching his boys about entrepreneurial success.

1. When you are introduced on stage, what is the most important thing you want people to know about you?

I want people to know that I'm a great father, husband and friend. I have an absolute 'can do' attitude and I love life.

2. What is your short cancer story?

In 2015, I was diagnosed with Colon cancer. After surgery and six months of chemo, I was labelled as 'in remission'. In February 2018, after a routine CT scan, I was told that it had come back with vengeance. It had spread to my lungs, and a few other areas. I am now in the fight to reach my goal of 'DRIVING MY CHILDREN'S CHILDREN TO SCHOOL'. At least. :)

3. When you were first diagnosed, how was your mental health and what did you do to keep going?

I was shocked. My wife and I couldn't believe it. We grieved on and off for a day or two and then we focused on me getting better. Attitude was our path. My wife and I were fortunate that for many years prior to this 'curveball', we spent a lot of time doing personal development work. I strongly believe that this was our key to mental health and sanity.

4. What business/work were you doing before you got sick and how was this affected?

Life has a funny way of testing us every step of the way. The difference between sitting in the corner and rocking back and forth, or LIVING, is a simple choice. At the same time as I was initially diagnosed, I was made redundant from my long-time career as a leading senior automotive designer. I had spent 20 years working directly and indirectly for GM Holden. Now, it was time to find a new career and battle cancer. See? Choice. I took this on as an opportunity to have a new, exciting career. I took all the skills I had, and all the passions that I wanted to pursue and found User Experience Design. Over the next year, I self-taught through online courses, attending meetups and more to immerse myself in this new world. I even managed to get a few interviews. However, the chemo schedule was interfering. Following that year, I completed a full-time course and started my new amazing career as a, now, Senior User Experience Designer with Telstra digital.

5. Was there a financial burden on you and your family when you got sick? Did you need to keep working?

The burden was enormous. I couldn't work for an entire year but the bills and the established way of life continued no matter what. We had to seriously dig into our property equity. I started my first job 18 months after my diagnosis. I did however do part-time jobs. Delivering food, helping out with some engineering where I could. But that was peanuts.

6. During treatment, what did you do to keep optimistic?

I focused on getting better. Learning my new career and immersing myself into that culture. I spent more time with the family and allowed my wife more time by taking care of the house.

7. How did you change your health routine once you were diagnosed?

Had I known then what I know now, I would have done even more. Back then, I eliminated sugar, milk, and processed foods. These were just basics. This was hard for someone that was a Russian who grew up with bread, milk, processed cold meats, lots of potatoes and a huge chocoholic. I continued with sports and exercise.

8. After treatment what parts of your life did you have to change or improve?

The most important part was negativity. I believe removing all negativity and negative reaction to circumstances is the key to healing. Unfortunately, I didn't master it the first time.

9. After treatment, how did your working/business life change?

I was forced into looking for a new career when the automotive industry was shutting down. In a way, I think I was fortunate in that I had to focus on something major at the same time that I was going through the cancer battle. I had a mission to requalify and once again be able to provide for my family.

10. What are your top 5 recommendations for people going through treatment?

- Attitude

- Gut health

- Nutrition

- Knowledge of what cancer is

- Allow others to help you – let your family and friends in

11. What are your top 5 recommendations for people after treatment who want to rebuild their physical, mental and financial health?

- "Remission" doesn't mean it's gone

- Continue focusing on nutrition and diet

- Connect with nature

- Exercise

- Focus on long-term financial goals

JO ROSS

Jo is a two-time survivor of Breast Cancer and runs her own business from Tasmania in the Summer and from her caravan traveling around Australia the rest of the year. She inspires people to live life on their terms and be happy.

1. When you are introduced on stage, what is the most important thing you want people to know about you?

I'm just a normal, average woman who decided to go for it.

2. What is your short cancer story?

I was diagnosed in 2012 with triple negative stage 2 Invasive Ductal Carcinoma just after my 33rd birthday. My cancer was not based on a hormone imbalance, nor was it genetic. It was just my body's way of saying, "Hey, you need to start looking after yourself better."

3. When you were first diagnosed, how was your mental health and what did you do to keep going?

I was completely miserable in my life before cancer. I was so lonely in my marriage and lived a life of walking on eggshells, never knowing what the next day would bring. I was living in survival mode and my only joy in life was my horses, donkeys and dogs. After the shock of my diagnosis wore off and I started to do some research about why a fairly healthy, non-smoking, slim, 33-year-old would get cancer, I began to realise how much our diet, emotions and our mental state affect our whole body's health. I threw myself into learning as much as I could about how to look after myself properly and became determined to not only survive this chapter of my life, but to thrive afterwards.

4. What business/work were you doing before you got sick and how was this affected?

I was working in a high-pressure and high-stress administration role. I loved my workmates but the work itself was not something I loved or was passionate about.

Because I chose a combination of natural and conventional treatment methods, I started out with taking two months unpaid leave while I underwent treatment, but during that time, so much changed within my relationship and within myself that I ended up resigning, selling our house and moving town.

5. Was there a financial burden on you and your family when you got sick? Did you need to keep working?

I had been the sole income provider for me and my now ex-husband for many years, so there was that pressure in the back of my mind of "what will we do?" Ultimately, we decided to sell our property, downsize and try to make life simpler. Our marriage survived less than a year after my diagnosis.

6. During treatment, what did you do to keep optimistic?

My diagnosis is what introduced me to the world of personal development. Many health books also offer incredible life wisdom, advice and inspiration for those looking for it, and this was me. These books and websites gave me so much hope, inspiration and laughs on my healing journey.

7. How did you change your health routine once you were diagnosed?

Everything changed for me. I did a 5-week juice diet in which my lump shrunk to half its size. I then had a lumpectomy to remove what was left of my tumour along with two lymph nodes to make sure the cancer had not spread. I then stuck faithfully to a high alkaline diet for the next three years and remained cancer free.

I then met my new husband and got completely blasé about my cancer and went back to eating everything and anything and drinking alcohol regularly. Sure enough, 12 months later (two days after my wedding) my cancer came back in exactly the same spot even more aggressively. After having a mastectomy in December 2016, needless to say, I am now back on my high alkaline diet and will be sticking to it.

8. After treatment what parts of your life did you have to change or improve?

Cancer and my marriage breakdown were catalysts for massive change. I took the time to cry, grieve and heal from my old life and really spend time thinking about who I was, who I wanted to be and what I wanted my life to look like.

9. After treatment, how did your working/business life change?

After my separation from my husband, I studied Early Childhood Education and started my own Family Day Care business thinking that owning my own business would give me the time and financial freedom I wanted in life. Boy was I wrong, lol. Two and half years later, I started in Network

Marketing as a side business to help bring in some extra income. In less than 12 months my side business was earning me more than my traditional business so I was able to close down my Day Care. As my income increased, my hubby was able to retire at age 49, we bought ourselves our dream 4wd and caravan and have been travelling around Australia ever since. We fell in love with a gorgeous 100-year-old cottage in Tasmania which we have bought as a summer home and will travel the rest of Australia each winter.

10. What are your top 5 recommendations for people going through treatment?

- Do your research, ask lots of questions, take notes, ask others what they have done. Get 2nd, 3rd and 4th opinions.

- Read, follow and watch Crazy, Sexy Kris Carr

- Read The PH Miracle by Dr Robert Young

- Try to find the gifts in your diagnosis. It may sound strange if you are newly diagnosed and are still being swept along on your whirlwind cancer journey, but there will be gifts in this journey and you can choose to find them, use them and grow a new beautiful life from them.

- Follow your own path. You will have many options

and many choices and not everyone will agree with what you decide to do, you will have to be ok with that. Your confidence will give others confidence.

11. What are your top 5 recommendations for people after treatment who want to rebuild their physical, mental and financial health?

- Don't wait. Figure out who you are, who you want to be and then find a way to make that happen. This is an ever-evolving process, but start now.

- Don't settle. It takes incredible courage to make big changes in your life, but you are absolutely worth it. Being loved for who you are is truly the greatest joy in life.

- Surround yourself with like-minded people. Whether that is in online communities, through books, clubs, Facebook groups, webinars, local support groups or email newsletters from people who are already where you want to be. You become like the 5 people you spend time around the most so choose wisely.

- Self-care. After your journey, and when life gets back to 'normal', it can be so easy to fall back into bad habits. Bad food choices, too much alcohol, habits that don't serve you and your health. Your body gave you a warning that you deserve better, learn from it and make looking after yourself a priority. It's not selfish, its necessary. You can't help anyone else if you're not around.

- I highly recommend network marketing as a fantastic business model to help you rebuild your financial and mental health. If you find a company and products that align with your values and that you truly believe in and can share from the heart, you will have found a way of earning an income that provides time freedom, location freedom, and financial freedom that will help you live life to the fullest.

"My cancer scare changed my life. I'm grateful for every new, healthy day I have. It has helped me prioritize my life."

- Olivia Newton-John

DEDICATION

To all my incredible Chemo Angels – thank you from the bottom of my heart. You not only helped me but you were there for my family, which I will be forever grateful for. Thank you Anthony, Jill, Val, Ria, Frank, Mark, Ann, Ken, Olya, Geoff, Michelle, Tanya, Brad, Shaye, Kim, Shane, Alex, Morgan, Chris, Chris, Vicki, Jenny, Pete, Terana, Bobbi, Ruth, Justin, Kelly, Bruce, Liz, Mike, Fiona, Angela, Mike, Liz, Deb, Phillippa, Daniele, Kim, Soph, Jac, Chick, Tree, Shay, Jason, Helen, Angela, Lorraine, John, Nicole, Ren, Merran, Kelly, Di, Simone, Brett, Leanne, Rebecca, Sue, Laura, Grace, Pene, Rachel, Tamara, Tina, Franck, Dr Di Viana, Dr Slancar and all the incredible nurses at Pindara and Icon especially Fern and Angela. And to my five beautiful Survivors who agreed to be interviewed – you are awesome humans.

To Peter and Sam – you inspire me every day. I am so proud of you.

Thank you also to my Editor, Emily Cox and Cover Designer, Pam Brossman. Thank you Pam for encouraging me to write this book and for providing a great platform for me to learn.

ABOUT MEGAN WOLFENDEN

Megan Wolfenden is an award-winning businesswoman who travels the world teaching people how to build their own businesses and reach their full potential. She is passionate about education and inspiring people to retire from their jobs and create a successful business for themselves and their families. She is also an Amazon #1 Bestselling Author. Her first book is called "Extraordinary You – A Woman's Guide to Having it All".

Megan started her career in banking, finance and the computer industry before relocating from Sydney, Australia, to the USA. She built a real estate portfolio, invested in gas, oil, gold, venture capital and other assets, and learnt about Network Marketing. Her multi-million-dollar distribution business operates out of 23 countries. She specializes in teaching Leadership and values-based goal setting and believes that results come through persistently and consistently working on your goals and enjoying the journey.

Days after her 50th Birthday, Megan was diagnosed with Breast Cancer and she is currently 12 months into her recovery journey. Megan is now also a Business and Health Coach, helping others prosper through life's challenging times.

Megan's previous book "Extraordinary You – A Woman's Guide to Having it All" is available through Amazon and online book stores globally.

If you are going through or have been through cancer and you are in need of a coach to help you get your life back on track, or simply to put the tools and techniques from this book into practise, contact Megan through her website at https://meganwolfenden.com

Her courses include:

- Happiness 101

- Extraordinary You

- Goals to Greatness

IMPORTANT LINKS

Australian Cancer Council

American Cancer Society

Your free Goal Setting Workbook and Strategy Session

---

*Life has a funny way of testing us every step
of the way. The difference between sitting
in the corner and rocking back and forth, or
LIVING, is a simple choice.*

– Alex Liberman

---

www.ingramcontent.com/pod-product-compliance
Lightning Source LLC
Chambersburg PA
CBHW072150020426
42334CB00018B/1944